MW00414962

SERVICE!
My Way of Life

By Mark J. Lindquist and Jared L. Bye

To order additional copies of this book or for more information on other Breath Is Limited Motivational Speaking products and services, contact us at www.BreathIsLimited.com.

Service! My Way of Life. Copyright © 2015 by Mark J. Lindquist and Jared L. Bye, First Edition. All rights reserved.

Inquiries regarding permission for the use of the material contained in this book should be addressed to Breath Is Limited Motivational Speaking, 3120-Z 25th St. South, Suite 160, Fargo, ND 58103.

Breath Is Limited Motivational Speaking, LLC

Look for these books by Mark J. Lindquist and Jared L. Bye coming soon!

- They! The Most Influential Group In America

- Failure! Don't Be Afraid Of It

- Dreams! The Biggest Thing You Should Own

- Action! The Time Is Now

- Priorities! Putting First Things First

- Goals! Knock Them Out of the Park

- Time! Owning It Is Priceless

SERVICE! My Way of Life

Dedicated to:

Becky Parker
Kyle Inforzato
Don Donais
Jerome Goddard
Magic Johnson
Heidi Bucher
Gordon and Diane Lindquist

Introduction

In this book I share with you my perspectives on the realm of service and volunteerism in America, which have been shaped by my experiences giving back to communities in every state in the nation and many countries all over the world. Since 1997, I have had the good fortune to live a life dedicated to the service of others and the betterment of the world around me.

I was given an early example of what it is to be a volunteer by my wonderful parents; without them, I wouldn't be able to write this book. Mom, who was/is a constant presence in the community of Ortonville, Minnesota; dad, who taught me how to extend myself beyond the borders of my hometown through his example of being a Peace Corps volunteer in his twenties; and my sister, Heidi, who without her guidance toward a service organization in high school, I wouldn't have had the journey I now claim as my own.

Seventeen years later with service in Clinton's AmeriCorps; years of membership in various service organizations such as Kiwanis, Lions, Jaycees and Rotary; community engagement roles with the Department of Homeland Security; nonprofit experience in dozens of communities throughout America; working with corporate community involvement departments at Fortune 500 companies with ties to White House charitable initiatives; six years of service in the United States Military giving back to communities and military installations in 124 locations all over the planet; and a passion to help grow service and volunteerism throughout our nation… I bring you this book.

My hope is that this book will spark an idea in your head and in your heart to increase your commitment to serve in your own community for the good of your neighbor and your nation. My hope is that this body of work will inspire someone in your life, possibly a young person, to reach out and give back to those who have given so much to them. My hope is that through these words you will be inspired to join me on a journey I call…

Service! My Way of Life.

Your Friend,
Mark J. Lindquist

By virtually every conceivable measure, social capital has eroded steadily and sometimes dramatically over the past two generations.

Robert D. Putnam

AUTHOR, *BOWLING ALONE*

Chapter 1: Putnam's Bowling Alone

In the fall of 1999, I sat in Memorial Auditorium at Concordia College's campus in Moorhead, MN and listened to a brilliant man named Robert Putnam. Putnam wrote the groundbreaking book titled, "Bowling Alone" which was being released to the public at the time. During his talk, he exposed me to the idea that civic engagement was on the decline over the course of generations since the '40s, '50s and '60s. By using the concept of after-work bowling leagues, he explained to the audience that we as a society used to meet up at the local bowling alley for a social gathering amongst members of the community; that we used to sit on our front porch and wave to our neighbors across the street and shout hello to the cars passing by. As his talk went on, he explained how those instances of bowling leagues and front porch meetings had declined drastically over the last three decades to the point where he felt that America was experiencing an epidemic in its social constructs that must be remedied by my generation (my words, not his).

Putnam cites study after study and poll after poll that illustrates the decline in participation in many of the traditional measuring sticks of social engagement. For example, he offers commentary on all types of participation – political, civic, religious, associations, philanthropic engagement – and he explains how virtually every metric is on the decline over the course of the latter half of the 20th century.

The country is now "Bowling Alone." I sat there in my seat and was absolutely enthralled by every conclusion he was offering to the audience at Concordia College that day. My generation, the generation who would later be labeled "The Millennials" was to face a social challenge that the previous generations had not: How to rebuild civic engagement in America.

Our generation of millennials (a.k.a. Generation Y), roughly defined as being born from 1980 to the early 2000s, would be handed a society in which participation in civically-minded activities wasn't perceived in the same way as it was in generations past. We grew up in a world with flashy demands on our time. First, it was the Sony Walkman that disengaged us from those around our personal bubble. Next, it was your dad's first Motorola bag phone, followed soon thereafter by Netscape, AOL and this crazy idea of a search engine called, "WebCrawler." The distractions included the personal computer, something called a mouse that wasn't actually a rodent and a new addition to our lexicon called "the World Wide Web." Think about the last time you used the phrase "World Wide Web." About that time your email address ended in hotmail.com, your CD player was playing the Spice Girls and you had to press the number 7 an excruciating four times if you wanted to text the letter "s".

Yes, my generation had made progress. We had left baggy backwards pants and big bangs in the past, but we were unaware of the challenges that our advancement through the technological age would bring. As we retreated into the Googling that replaced asking questions and having conversations, we were also ignoring calls only to text the caller a few seconds later. For every benefit of a Wikipedia search and having the whole of human knowledge at the touch of a button; we spent three hours of our leisure time staring at videos of cats and obsessing about the next level in Angry Birds when we could've been engaging with others in our community.

The competition for our time and attention is fiercer than any other moment in history. Rare is the conversation over three minutes that isn't interrupted by a glance at a cell phone screen or a quick text sent with one hand beneath the table, pretending our audience doesn't see what we're doing. This chapter isn't meant to be an indictment of technology or its role in modern society. Rather, I simply want to call attention to the challenges we all face to carve out time in our busy, distracted lives to volunteer, participate and engage.

I believe now more than ever, we live in a society that wants to hear the answer to the question, "What's in it for me?" I'm not suggesting that the young generation or society as a whole has become more selfish or comes from a position that reflects a need to be benefited first. I'm simply noting that in order for one thing to take precedence over another in our busy lives, there has to be a compelling answer to the question, "What's in it for me?" Take this for example: We all have 168 hours in a week. That's all we are given and nobody gets more and nobody is given less. 168 hours. In America, we now live in a society where a growing majority of households have two working adults. My observation on the state of children in America is that more and more we're asking our kids to specialize earlier, commit to a sport or other extracurricular at younger and younger ages because the competition is becoming tougher and tougher as the years go. We're asking our young people to do well in preschool so they get into the right kindergarten; do well in elementary school so they can be accepted into the right middle school and on and on and on. My observation is that if we aren't careful, we'll be tying a child's kindergarten performance to their eventual acceptance into Harvard.

What does this mean when it comes to civic engagement?

Simple. There is seemingly more pressure to perform well and score high; there are a bevy of activities and lessons to engage our children and families in, and thus we feel "busier" than we have ever been. This busy life creates a challenge when we're trying to "fit in" a volunteer activity or association meeting into our weekly and monthly calendar. We have trended toward a "me and mine" focus when it comes to our calendar – pick up Johnny, drop off Junior. Attend Sally's play and then it's off to Billy's recital. In the midst of all the hustle, community involvement is typically the loser.

We're a busy group of people. As Putnam notes, all of these things are ingredients in the formula that has resulted in the decline of social engagement in America. Putnam wrote the book, "Bowling Alone" 15 years ago, so my assumption is the challenges he mentions are only larger and more influential in the year 2015.

My generation has a responsibility to recognize and change this trend. In order to do that, we will examine what I believe is a system which served its purpose and now must evolve if it is to survive the first half of the 21st century. The system I refer to is the service club universe, and we will dive deeper into that realm in the next chapter.

*The day we make impacting another's life
through your time, energy, ideas or actions
as interesting as the next level of Angry Birds —
then we have made real progress in the realm
of service in America.*

Mark J. Lindquist

Chapter 2: The Service Club Universe

I grew up in the service clubs. In my hometown of Ortonville, Minnesota, I was involved during my sophomore year of high school in an organization called "Key Club." At the time, it was the largest high school service organization in the world with over 250,000 members. This club was sponsored by a civic organization called Kiwanis. I got my start in clubs like the Ortonville Kiwanis Club. I attended meetings; I spoke at clubs; I visited neighboring communities, bringing news of our service to them and exchanging ideas about how to best serve our local area. Without Key Club and specifically, the Kiwanians of Ortonville and the Minnesota-Dakotas District of Kiwanis International, I wouldn't be writing this book today. More importantly, without them, I wouldn't have lived a life dedicated to the service of others these past 17 years.

Since I left Ortonville, Minnesota at the age of 18 (15 years ago), I have been a member of Kiwanis Clubs, Lions Clubs, Jaycees and Rotary in communities all over the nation. I have attended meetings of various civic organizations such as these in dozens and dozens of communities all over the country. I love the people. I am impressed by the work that is done through these organizations. I am blown away by the giving hearts and spirits of the members of these fine institutions.

However, they must change.

As I travel around the nation to speak to various service organizations, the conversation is always the same, whether the banner at the front of the room says Lions, Kiwanis or Rotary. The conversation amongst the leadership of these large service organizations is about their strategy for survival past the year 2040.

The Kiwanis International website states that the average member is 55.1 years old. If you've been in the rooms that I've been in around the service club universe, that number seems pretty consistent across the various organizations. Suffice to say, when I go speak to a service club during their weekly meeting, the audience I look out upon has a lot of gray hair. Aging membership of these service clubs is a real concern, and if these organizations don't take some sort of massive, determined action (thanks for the phrase, Tony Robbins) to ensure their survival into the next generation, they will find themselves next to the Dodo Bird and the Saber Toothed Tiger on the extinct species list. Any service organization that doesn't pay close attention to this generational recruitment problem is, in my estimation, already on the endangered species list.

How do you attract new, young members to an old-school service club? This is the question many of the forward thinking club leaders must be asking themselves across the nation and world. The one challenge I see industry-wide is club leadership fails to recognize the accuracy of the latter portion of that question: "old-school service club."

Now, before I continue, I implore club leaders of all levels to take their heart off their sleeve and hear me out on my ideas. I have been developing these ideas over the course of the past 15+ years, and they are my attempt to "be the change I wish to see in the world." They are my ideas only, and they are not tried and true. Far be it from me to challenge the age-old traditions of civic organizations that have millions of members worldwide and raise hundreds of millions of dollars annually to support causes and communities around the planet. These are just the thoughts and observations of a kid who grew up in this system, is a product of it and possibly considered by some to be a "success story" of the modern civic club-sponsored youth programs. All I am is a guy who has an idea about how to change the system for the benefit of our future generations.

"Old-school service club" – that's what it is. Generally, these organizations initially began as a means for businessmen to gather and network, exchange business and better their communities. It was a brotherhood of men, so to speak. Some came right out of the gates with a service-oriented mission; others began as a means to gain a sort of group insurance benefit in the gathering of businessmen. Many of the great service clubs we know today started anywhere from the late 1800s to the early 1900s.

No matter the origin, the evolution of the service club has produced a fairly homogeneous structure in today's society – weekly meetings officiated by elected club officers where a meal is enjoyed and business of the organization is conducted. The typical components on the agenda are: a guest speaker, various traditions of music, patriotism, sharing, fundraisers, and community project discussions.

This is my opinion of the state of the civic organization in 2015. In the year 2014, I was a member of both Kiwanis and Rotary. If I feel compelled to recruit a young member of our community to join our local service club, the primary outlet and "recruiting grounds" is that of a weekly club meeting.

So, here's my plan. I am going to recruit Bob. Bob is somewhere south of 30 years old. He's a young professional, probably married, probably a father and is an ambitious and talented young guy – otherwise I wouldn't necessarily think him a good fit for a tight-knit service organization like ours.

--

Outgoing text message:

Me: Hey Bob! I would love it if you'd join me at our next Rotary/Kiwanis/Lions/Insert Civic Org Here meeting.

Bob: Oooh, I'm pretty busy.

Me: No problem, we meet Tuesday's at Noon at the golf clubhouse. You gotta eat anyway, why don't you let me buy you lunch?

Bob: Well, when you put it that way I guess I can't refuse. Pick me up?

Me: Great, you'll love our club.

(Note subtle hints of recruitment already beginning. :-p)

--

Now if we're honest with ourselves... with the 30-and-under crowd, the exchange probably would have looked more like this:

--

Outgoing Text:

Me: lunch tues @ 12?

Bob: sry slammed

Me: my treat

Bob: sold

--

Now I've got Bob committed to a meeting with our club – Awesome. Bob has never been to a meeting of a civic organization, because, as we mentioned before, the demands on his time as a young husband and father are just too great. But nonetheless, at noon on Tuesday at the country club, Bob gets his first taste of the service club universe.
Enter the club meeting. For the most part, Bob feels like he just

stepped into a 1950s business meeting and is wondering if he should have worn his skinny black tie, fedora and brought his briefcase to this meeting. After singing songs of old from a tattered songbook straight out of an episode of black and white TV, he stands and says the pledge of allegiance for the first time since the 2nd grade. He sits through a meetings conducted with poorly executed parliamentary procedure while he chokes down stale dinner rolls and awkwardly passes the hat to his left as everyone else puts in a dollar and shares their "happy thoughts." During this process, he is left wondering if he missed the memo to stop at the ATM and get cash. After all of this, a subtle amount of pressure is placed on him to join the club after just one grueling meeting with people old enough to be his grandparents. He shrugs off the offer with a half-hearted smile and chuckle as he heads for the door. On his way out the door, the club president stops Bob and hands him a paper application for membership after telling him, "They really could use some new blood around here."

Bob was never seen or heard from again.

This scenario has played out week after week at service clubs in the nation for the last 20 years. "We can't seem to recruit younger members," club leaders say. Breakout sessions are offered at the Kiwanis/Lions/Rotary/Insert Service Club Here

District Conventions with titles such as, "How to Relate to Young Prospective Members," "How to Recruit to the Generation Y Population" and "Aging Club Membership... What to Do About It."

Why is it that organizations doing such great work in our communities have such a hard time recruiting new members?

We are a service club. We serve. We volunteer. We contribute to our community. This is why we exist.

However, we can't inspire people to love service as we do by making them attend a weekly meeting.

I want people to catch the bug of service. I want them to be motivated to serve and find time in their busy schedules to volunteer and give back to their community. But I can't motivate my fellow millennial to love service if my primary recruiting grounds for new membership is a weekly meeting. We already attend enough meetings in our professional careers. In today's working world we all attend dozens and dozens of meetings a month if we count conference calls, weekly team round-ups, pulling our chairs over to a neighbor's cubicle, outside conferences and gatherings... The last thing we want to do is use our free time during breakfast, lunch or happy hour to attend another boring meeting.

Now, I can't argue with the idea that gathering for a weekly meeting creates opportunities for building relationships with key members of the community. I won't argue that it is a great way to learn about new and exciting projects going from the guest speaker of the day.

However, here's the distinction I want to make: We are a **SERVICE** club. The only way to get someone hooked on service is to allow him or her to serve. Isn't that the goal with each new member of our organizations? The goal is to get members of our community and society to become hooked on service. We want to inspire them to live a life dedicated to the community. We want volunteerism to take precedence in this person's life. We want them to become a champion of a cause or an organization that is near and dear to their heart. We want them to live the values of our organization we recite before every weekly meeting.

However, our primary recruiting grounds and primary recruiting strategy is to bring a new millennial to an archaic meeting that doesn't inspire. It may inform… but informing is a far cry from inspiring. Consider the following quote (next page):

If you are going to become addicted to service...
Attending a weekly service club meeting is not
considered an enabler.

Mark J. Lindquist

If our desire is for people to become addicted to service, a meeting is not the place to accomplish this goal. With this current system, we end up with club membership that is part of an organization for reasons other than service. Certainly, a portion of the people are there out of a love for service and volunteerism, but the remainder of the membership roster is there for a variety of other reasons: Maybe it looks good on their resume. Maybe their employer told them they had to join such a service club and wear the company nametag to every event. Maybe it is a social event or a networking opportunity. Maybe attendance at the meeting allows a person to lead and shine for the only time in an otherwise average week. Maybe it is the way one has the chance to get to know a community they just arrived in.

These "other" reasons for membership result in a community service chair constantly relying on the same six people to get the service project done. This membership composition results in 82 people on a membership roster and 24 people consistently showing up to meetings. People will move heaven and earth in their busy schedules to attend something they're passionate about, and most people I know aren't passionate about attending a weekly meeting.

If service clubs truly exist to serve, then we need to let the people serve. In Robert Putnam's book "Bowling Alone," he references research that states:

> [1] "Measured in terms of hours per month, the average American's investment in organizational life (apart from religious groups, which we shall examine separately) fell from 3.7 hours per month in 1965 to 2.9 in 1975 to 2.3 in 1985 and 1995."

I only have so many hours in my month to dedicate to an organization or community effort. The simple truth is that I'm busy like the rest of the world. If the statistic above holds true in my life – I'm spending two to four hours a month attending a service club meeting, and my life falls in line with the national average – that leaves me with approximately zero hours to engage in direct service.

We make our people attend weekly meetings and give awards to the people who never miss a meeting because we suspend membership for those who don't regularly attend meetings – we are cannibalizing our own mission. If we make someone attend a regular meeting in order to be a member of the club, then we have guaranteed only the above-average member will find the time to engage in the actual service projects planned at the meeting.

Examine the statistics: If 2.3 hours per month are spent inside or-ganizational life, then few will find time above and beyond to serve at the projects your club has planned. This is precisely why 80 percent of the work is done by 20 percent of the club membership. You have statistically set yourself up for such an outcome because of this experience I call "service fatigue." The club leadership is constantly leaning on the same six people to do the work – year after year it wears on a person. This is the same reason why each and every club I have ever attended is running club officer elections unopposed. Unless you're an ambitious young college student fresh into the workforce, the average club member avoids the responsibility of being a club officer until finally "it's my turn."

The next generation doesn't have time to engage in something it isn't passionate about. For most, club meetings – attending them and running them – becomes a chore, not a passion.
If we are open to the fundamental restructuring of our service clubs in America and beyond, take heed to the wise words of the great American father himself, Mr. Benjamin Franklin:

Tell me and I forget, teach me and I may remember, **involve me** *and I learn.*

Benjamin Franklin

My friends, we must involve our members and prospective members in direct service. We must give them the opportunity right out of the gates to look into the eyes of those we serve and catch the bug of volunteer service. According to their 2013 study on volunteerism in the United States, the Bureau of Labor Statistics states that teens (16-19 year olds) had a volunteer rate of 26.2 percent.

This means once you get them engaged at your service club when they're in their '20s, over 70 percent of the young people you invite to your club haven't had any experience volunteering in the community.

YOU may be the sole exposure a young person has to the world of volunteerism and community service. Don't waste that golden opportunity on a meeting. At a meeting you're employing the strategy Ben Franklin speaks of: "Tell me and I forget." That young person is going to walk out of the meeting and forget about the service your club president or service chair spoke of. If we involve our prospective members, then we have a shot at opening their eyes to the world of service enough to want to commit to membership.

As a salesman, I have long lived by the old adage "You have to connect before you pull." I think this applies to club membership. We're selling something, my friends. We're selling comradery; we're selling impact; we're selling fun. Make no mistake, as recruiters for club membership we are salespeople. Where do you think club dues come from? Sure, some companies value service club membership enough to pay for an employee's club dues – but the hundreds of dollars per year that a member of a service organization has to pay comes from somewhere. The prospective member has to be sold on the idea that membership is worth spending hard earned dollars on. A young person just starting out in his or her career may be tight on money, and those dollars for club dues might not be high on the priority list next to diapers, gas in the tank and clothes to wear to the new job. We have to sell them on the idea. I speak as a salesman yet again – I simply don't think in that in this transaction, a weekly meeting is our best value proposition.

--

So, I have spent the last 1,700+ words bashing the traditional club meeting in the service club universe. If you're still with me after all of that, you're probably wondering what Mr. Smarty-Pants Author thinks the solution is. Here it is, my friends. It's an idea that I have been tossing back and forth in my mind for the last

15+ years since I engaged with the Kiwanis organization and their sponsored youth program called Key Club in 1997. You may say, "Well, that's all nice 'pie-in-the-sky' talk, and any idea can sound good on paper, but who is to say your ideas won't fall flat?"

They might. They just might be the worst ideas that ever saw the light of day. But the difference is, I have ideas about how to change things. I have ideas on how we must evolve in order to survive past the year 2040. I have ideas about how to be the change I wish to see in the world. This is my release party. This is my launch. You are my launchpad. Maybe my solutions need more work. Maybe my ideas will need to be changed once they are enacted in "the real world." Great. Awesome. Let's do it.

I'm a small town kid who owes his start in life to a Kiwanis Club and a sponsored youth organization called Key Club. My desire for life is that I can do something to ensure that a new generation of young people who are born in the year 2025 and beyond have the opportunity to experience a life hooked on service as I have.

---

1. Robert D. Putnam, *Bowling Alone: The Collapse and Revival of American Community.* (New York: Simon & Schuster, 2000), 62.

Don't believe that the system that was handed to you is the best system, simply because it was handed to you.
What if there was a better way?

Mark J. Lindquist

Chapter 3: Service Clubs – My Solution for the Future

Fundamental restructuring of service clubs in America – That's my goal.

Bold?

Yes.

Brave?

Definitely.

Possible?

Well, that depends on you.

At all the regional, division and district conventions I have been to, I have yet to hear anyone with the guts to stand up and say what I'm saying. Nobody to my knowledge has laid out a plan and a vision for how our civic organizations will evolve in order to not only survive for generations, but once again thrive in the heart of our demographics.

Service Club Universe, allow me to unveil my plan for the future.

As with every good plan, my plan has points – three to be exact – and they are:

1. Eliminate Club Meetings
2. Replace Club Meetings with Direct Service Projects
3. Reorganize Club Officer Structure

There you have it. This is my solution for a more robust club membership of the future. This is my solution for a service club value proposition that will make sense in the face of today's busy two-income professional household. This is my solution to ensure that we are relevant for the next generation and beyond. It is an evolution that must take time and be embraced by a new and forward-looking leadership team. Today's membership will reject it. This isn't "the way we've always done it." But you and I both know, in order to survive for more then the next 25 years, our clubs cannot possibly continue to conduct "business as usual." A new generation of civic leaders shall lead us into the middle part of this century, and we must develop a system that fits into their busy lives and is an attractive part of their list of priorities.

1. Eliminate Club Meetings

If you didn't see this coming when you read the previous chapter, I really think I must stink as a communicator.

It's simple math. If busy professionals with a spouse and kids live with both parents working, then their lives are busier and demands on their time are greater. And, if distractions of television and technology continue to threaten the available hours left a person has to dedicate to the betterment of one's community, then we must respond with an opportunity to engage with our service clubs in a way that: A) inspires people, and B) causes our event on their calendar to rise to the top of their many priorities.

If the average person has three hours a month to dedicate to a community-related cause, and those three hours are spent at a weekly meeting, then we are denying the majority of membership the opportunity to get out in the community and serve. If we want to get people hooked on service, let them serve. I didn't catch the bug of volunteer service because I had the chance to attend a weekly Key Club meeting at 7:45 a.m. in the high school library. I got hooked on service because I got to look into the eyes of a homeowner whose house we just saved from rising floodwaters because we cared enough to get out there and sandbag in the freezing cold spring rain. I didn't get hooked on service because I got to conduct a conference call and officiate a board meeting. I got hooked on service because I got to see the tears of the family whose house was just blown to pieces by an F4 tornado in St. Peter, Minnesota and take part as 52 high school students showed up to help with the cleanup and recovery efforts.

As an institution, we have to remember one thing: Service is the reason we are here. We need to invite prospective members to direct service projects preferably where the new member is allowed to interact directly with those affected by our work. Certainly, there are projects on our list that are more of a support function or back-office work. Those are projects that should be reserved for the long-time faithful who understand the value of the work being completed by volunteers. You should reserve direct service projects like building a house for Habitat for Humanity, tutoring an underprivileged student, disaster relief, homeless shelter support, wounded warrior support/care, etc. for the new recruits. Remember, the majority of your new prospective members haven't volunteered in the community prior to showing up on your worksite. Provide them with a lasting and memorable experience that will keep them coming back for more. Allow them to see firsthand the impact of their work **on people**, not just on the organization.

2. Replace Club Meetings with Direct Service Projects

I was a member of AmeriCorps and served proudly with them for two and a half years in Washington, D.C. as we performed volunteer work in 13 states throughout the mid-Atlantic. We worked in teams of 10-14 people and were paired with a local nonprofit organization that needed some good old-fashioned "people power" around their community. Sometimes it was down and dirty labor that wasn't something the organization had the capacity to complete; sometimes it was something way down on the nonprofit's wish list that never seemed to get done because there were many other priorities taking precedence. Regardless of the type of activity, we knew that with our youthful people power showing up in force for 6-8 weeks at a time, we were empowering nonprofits all over the nation to better accomplish their missions by taking some of the pressure off of the already stretched-thin staff at the organization.

Most of the time, we were tasked to accomplish ancillary projects that the nonprofit staff would have otherwise had to dedicate valuable time and resources, thus, taking them away from their primary organizational mission. It was the mission and vision of AmeriCorps to send hard-working teams of young volunteers to accomplish an organization's "wish-list" items while freeing up the trained nonprofit staff to dive deeper into the tasks and projects requiring their expertise.

One such example occurred in Franklin, West Virginia while working with a local Habitat for Humanity affiliate in Pendleton County. The small staff of four at this local affiliate had long wished to open a Habitat for Humanity "Re-Store," whereby a local affiliate would run a used furniture and hardware store in order to establish additional revenue for the organization. The concept is simple: donations of furniture and construction related supplies are sought from the community; items are then sold at a reduced price to the community and all proceeds return back to the local Habitat for Humanity affiliate. It's a great addition to any Habitat affiliate, and those who have the capacity to get a re-store up and running are at a tremendous advantage.

For this affiliate, the four staff (two construction supervisors and two office staff) were so busy trying to accomplish their mission of providing a simple, decent place to live for local residents who qualified for their homes, they never seemed to have time to dedicate resources and hours to the opening of the re-store. What needed to happen was the demolition and modest remodeling of a commercial space previously donated to them. Then, a press release campaign would need to be launched, informing the general public that the Habitat re-store was accepting donations, and community members could now shop there.

Our AmeriCorps team was the perfect fit for the re-store project. We could storm into town for eight weeks and perform the demo and remodel while the trained nonprofit staff maintained their day-to-day duties – their mission never suffered. A net good was achieved because, at the end of the project, the affiliate had a new source of revenue, and they never had to "take their eye off the ball" when it came to their mission.

This is the type of support project I am suggesting you leave for your old faithful. Send your members that have been part of your club for the last 10 years and will always be stalwarts for your organization. This type of project, which requires a greater understanding of how the work impacts an organization, should be reserved for the 20 percent of your membership you would constantly lean on to ensure the work gets done. Pairing this type of member with this project is a key component of organizational success because the member does not become de-motivated for lack of understanding on how their work impacts the organization, and it keeps the people engaged in direct service, which is the whole purpose of the club.

--

The next type of project is one I would offer to new recruits and prospective members. With the same organization – Habitat for Humanity – I offer this example:

We were building a house for the Fort Lauderdale Habitat for Humanity affiliate in South Florida in the spring of 2002. We were leading volunteers who had enrolled in Habitat's "Collegiate Challenge" spring break program. As we were building a house for a family of five, we learned their current situation wasn't ideal – family of five, living in a small one-bedroom apartment. There wasn't much room for three young kids in a stuffy Fort Lauderdale apartment. We were working on the house during the very early stages of construction – stud walls still exposed, windows barely hung, exposed concrete everywhere, roof barely sheeted.

One day, the mother of the family pulled up on the worksite with her 4-year-old son. The little boy leaped out of the car when he saw me and ran to my side. He exclaimed with the joy and excitement of a little 4-year-old boy, "Mark! Mark! Come here!" He grabbed my hand tightly and ran me inside the house. As we rushed down what was to be a hallway and arrived at the thresh-old of what was to be a bedroom, he shouted with glee, "Look!

This is MY ROOM! And I get TWO WINDOWS!"
I looked down at that little boy and had the chance to see hope for the first time. Think of the hope and promise that were ahead for that little boy. He not only had a house; he now had a place he could call home. I was able to have that experience and see a child's life impacted forever because I was a volunteer.

This is the type of project I want you to send your new recruits on. I'm not saying that during each and every project you'll capture a moment or story like the one I had with the 4-year-old boy. However, if you put your new prospective members in those situations with a clear example of how their work is impacting other people in their community, then I believe you are setting up for success – success being defined by increasing the engagement of new members, members of our community, with the nonprofits and great causes in our local area.

--

What you'll do as you replace your regular club meetings with direct service projects is increase your likelihood of an individual becoming **inspired** by the work you do, thus, increasing the likelihood of them returning for a future project.

Recruit to these projects, not to a meeting. Hold a brief (BRIEF!) round up at the beginning and end of each direct service project, which can take the place of your regular club business meetings. Communicate the opportunities to serve, celebrate the service accomplished and dive into the project. Use five minutes max with the round up. Everything else can be communicated via email newsletter with all the pertinent information. Maximize a new recruit's time with you by letting them **engage in service** rather than just talk about service. Remember, "Tell me and I forget... Involve me and I learn."

Fellowship and relationships. Some may criticize my plan because they say that the club fellowship and relationships developed at club meetings are an integral part of club member experience. They might argue that the sense of belonging to a group is a necessary part of what a service organization provides its membership.

Ok, I will concede that point. However, tell me those relationships can't be forged while serving directly next to that prospective or current member. Certainly there are projects that exist in our portfolio during which little or no person-to-person interaction can be had for reasons of safety or wellbeing. However, I would venture to guess the vast majority of projects we would send our membership on provide a plethora of opportunities to get to know the person they are serving alongside. I contend that the relationship forged in the trenches of direct service are as good or better than the relationship forged while sitting next to someone in a weekly meeting.

Also, you must remember – by employing this direct service mentality, you will recruit a much different demographic that will one day dominate your membership roster. If you recall my previous assertion, many different people join service clubs for a multitude of reasons beyond altruistic service to their community. You will find that if your primary recruiting tool is a direct service experience, you will attract and retain a wholly different membership – hopefully one that is highly dedicated to the betterment of their community.

3. Club Officer Structure

The traditional roles of President, Vice President, Secretary/ Treasurer, etc. have less effect in a field-based organization that moves itself away from the typical "business meeting" structure we are used to. Although some of those roles might still be necessary in this new club format – specifically the club treasurer – I would focus most of the emphasis on the roles which move the club toward service and engagement in the community. For this reason, I propose four club officer roles for this new generation model of service club.

1. **Service Chair:** The person in this role is responsible for identifying the causes and projects the club will engage in during the week and hear from club members about which organizations the membership would like to support. This is the highest elected position in the club, because providing direct service is the most important part of our organization.

2. **Communications Director:** Since the club does not hold regular business meetings to communicate upcoming service opportunities, it is imperative that a communications director be in constant contact with the membership via email, e-newsletters and even mass text lists to communicate the next volunteer opportunity to the membership. As inclusion on the email list is the new threshold for a member in good standing, the club is able to have a broader reach of members by simple inclusion on the email blast and newsletter mailing list. For example, instead of sending out word of your projects to the 84 "members" you have on your roster – even though roughly 50 percent of those are "active members" – you now send your email notification out to 780 people who have once expressed

interest in volunteering for the causes you support, and you'll gain a much larger participation from a larger sample of your local population.

The role of the communications director also takes on another form when at the volunteer site. The communications director works closely with the event team (explained next) to ensure everyone in attendance at the volunteer worksite has a clear understanding of "why" they are doing the work they are doing. Because, as the brilliant man Stephen Covey says, "If you have a big enough WHY, you can live with any WHAT."

Throughout my experience leading over 15,000 volunteers all over the nation, I have found that the most important component of a successful volunteer experience is to know why I am doing what I am doing. If I am sitting in limbo on the sidelines of a project because x, y and z need to be accomplished before the volunteer workforce may resume their duties, then I need to communicate this to my volunteers. The fatal flaw of volunteer managers is that they keep the information to themselves and leave their most valuable resource to fend for themselves in the "hurry up and wait" realm. In this scenario, frustrations run high very quickly. As a communications director, I need to constantly be working with my event team to keep everyone in the loop about what is happening, why we are doing what we are doing and most importantly, paint the big picture of why our work matters to the organization we are volunteering for. When possible, the communications director arranges for a real live person affected by the work to be present and speak to the club membership to express their gratitude.

3. **Event Team:** The event team works closely with the service chair to organize the volunteer service projects the club decides to engage in. The event team includes the people power or "foot-soldiers" who make the projects happen and organize a successful volunteer experience. Nametags, refreshments, photo opportunities, facility or worksite orientation, volunteer task list, safety briefing, media relations, etc. – these are all tasks the event team would carry out under the direction and guidance of the service chair. The event team also arranges social gatherings for club members quarterly or annually in order to provide a fun and relaxing atmosphere for the club members to get to know one another.

4. **Fundraising Chair:** This person coordinates all fundraising efforts amongst the club membership.

With this streamlined club structure, the focus is and always will be direct service. Now, we all know that in our organizations there exists a "check-writing club." I'm not upset with them. They make the wheel go round. If you're in a check-writing club, then stay in the check-writing club. Hold your weekly meetings and write your checks. The nonprofit community needs you to continue to do what you do. I'm coming at this generational problem from a recruitment and sustainability perspective that will carry us into the middle part of the 21st century. But if you're a check-writing club, then you have found a niche in which you are able to recruit the right men and women to engage with you and support the causes you believe in financially – and that's fantastic.

This is my vision for the future of service clubs in America and around the world. I have cast that vision for you, and now it is up to the world to decide whether the ideas have merit. I am under no delusion that I have laid before you a perfectly conceived plan; however, after my experiences in the service club universe over the past 15+ years and careful consideration of these ideas throughout those years, I am proud to bring this vision to you. As Dr. Martin Luther King Jr. so wisely stated:

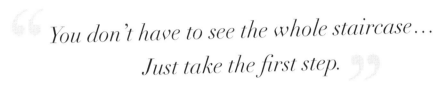

You don't have to see the whole staircase…
Just take the first step.

Dr. Martin Luther King Jr.

All a person really needs is someone to believe in them. If they have that... just watch what they can do.

Mark J. Lindquist

Chapter 4: Key Club, AmeriCorps and Mentorship

As a sophomore in high school, I was fortunate enough to get a ride to school from my older sister Heidi, who was a senior that year. I say I was fortunate because it was infinitely cooler to arrive at school in my sister's car than the school bus.

Every day, she would take me to school and probably run from her car the moment we parked in the parking lot, for fear of being associated with her kid brother for more than a few moments. However, on Thursday mornings, life was a little different. On Thursdays we would have to leave the farm extra early in order to arrive at the school for a 7:45 a.m. meeting. The meeting was for an extracurricular club Heidi was involved in. This club was called Key Club.

I had no idea what this was, and at first I would simply go to my locker and hang out before the bell rang at 8:20 a.m. Eventually, I decided to find out what was so interesting about making keys – what about this club would compel a high school senior to wake up early on a Thursday in order to complete this locksmith-related activity?

Much to my surprise, it had nothing to do with a literal interpretation of the name whatsoever. The kids who were part of Key Club weren't making keys at all – they were serving the community. As I soon learned, the "Key" in Key Club stood for "Kiwanis Educating Youth." A local Kiwanis Club in Ortonville, Minnesota had decided to establish a youth branch of their service organization, and they chartered a Key Club at my high school. They found an advisor and identified some leaders from my sister's class (including my sister Heidi), and they launched a community service club at Ortonville High School.

From those days forward, my life would never be the same. I don't know if I have ever recognized Heidi for paving the way for me. So please allow me to do that right now. Heidi, sis – Thank you for caring enough to set a positive example for me in my young life. The trail you blazed as the Class of 1996 at OHS was one that indirectly impacted my life for the next 17 years. Thank you for being a difference maker in my life and in the lives of countless others who have been impacted by the work of the Ortonville High School Key Club.

When I was growing up, I had a fantastic set of examples to learn from. My mother taught me that the Lindquist family was a family who gave back to others. The Lindquist family was a family who volunteered and contributed to the lives of our fellow community members whenever possible. There wasn't a church youth group bake sale, Girl Scout troop event or community effort that wasn't somehow supported by my mother, Diane Lindquist. She was constantly out there in the community alongside our long-time family friend Ronda Thielke doing her best to make a better life and better community for us kids and for the next generation. Whether they knew it or not – Mom and Ronda were setting an example for a kid like me. They were showing me that volunteerism was not just something engaged in every once in a while. They showed me that it was a way of life. For that, and for living the way you do – thank you for paving the way for a crazy kid like me. Because of your example, I instinctively knew what mattered in life and understood the value of service to others.

My father Gordon Lindquist is my real life hero. My dad was a traveler when he was in his twenties, and he managed to make the leap from small town farm kid of Ortonville (population 2,000) to world traveler and difference maker. A leap not many can say they have successfully taken. When my dad was at the University of Minnesota pursuing a degree in agriculture, he had this crazy idea that one day he would join Kennedy's Peace Corps. Not sure if a small town farm kid could hack it in the bush for two years in the program – he decided to study abroad in Germany for a year. His thinking was if he could make it in a civilized country where they didn't speak English (primarily), well then he just might be able to make it in the Peace Corps wherever they assigned him.

So dad ended up taking off on an adventure in the Peace Corps that took him westward from Ortonville, Minnesota to Malaysia for a two year assignment teaching the villagers how to farm. After his Peace Corps tour was over, he continued west from Malaysia and saw a movie in Tehran, Iran; spent Christmas Eve in Bethlehem; learned to ski in the Alps; hitchhiked across Europe; returned to the farm in Germany where he had lived and studied; boarded a ship in Rotterdam and sailed across the North Atlantic; landed in New York City; drove a car from New York to Milwaukee; and caught the train from Milwaukee to Ortonville. He had literally circled the globe in two and a half years.

My father showed me that there was a great big world out there, and I could see it if I wanted to. He is the reason why I love travel and adventure. He is the reason I dream big and reach for my audacious goals. He did it before me, and whether he knew it or not, the example of the life he lived was giving me a license to dream and achieve what others thought impossible.

Having had his example of serving others in the Peace Corps, of course I would choose to serve in AmeriCorps and eventually the

U.S. Military. Of course I would hold service as a value in my life. To my father, Gordon Lindquist – I cannot thank you enough for shaping who I am today and who I have been throughout my adult life. I am happy with "how I turned out." I am proud to follow in your footsteps. The very thought that I would live a life dedicated to serving others first started with your example. For this and countless other contributions to my young life, I thank you and love you for who you are.

You see, I was pretty darn lucky in my young life. I had three tremendous examples of how to live life in my sister, mom and dad. Aside from the family examples, I also was fortunate enough to have four other adults in my community who really believed in me and helped to propel me into the future. There were countless others beyond the four that I will mention here… but these four I must mention.

Becky Parker. Anyone who knows Becky Parker is better for it. She was the Kiwanis Advisor for our Key Club when I was in high school. Without Becky, I wouldn't be anywhere close to where I am today, and that's the truth. Becky showed me time after time what it was to commit to the community and show up when others wouldn't. She extended herself far beyond what was asked of her and was a constant reminder to me of what I could be. To my dear friend and mentor, Becky Parker – may the world be fortunate to have many more like you… and may those impacted by the Becky Parkers of the world be wise enough to know you have crossed paths with pure goodness. Thank you, Becky.

Kyle Inforzato. We call him "Coach I." Twenty years after meeting this man, I am still singing his praises. I may only see Coach once every decade or so, but I have thought of him probably once a week for the past 20 years. The man he is is who I aspire to be. If I had a nickel for every time Coach I was there for me when seemingly nobody else was… well, I'd have a barrel full of nickels. Coach I was a mentor to me who showed me what it was to stand up for myself and for what I believed in and be comfortable being me without apology. Coach I is a man who lives his life along the "extra mile," and each and every young person who comes in contact with him has a better shot at success in life than they did before. This past year, I had the good fortune to be able to express a small portion of my appreciation for his role in my life when I sang for the Minnesota Twins on Saturday, July 5th, 2014. We played host to the New York Yankees in front of a crowd of over 36,000 and the Twins were gracious enough to grant me a couple of field passes for some special guests.

Fifteen years earlier, I delivered my first rendition of the National

Anthem at the Ortonville High School Athletic Field for Coach I's football team. Fifteen years later, I had the opportunity to stand next to him as he and his wonderful wife Bonnie joined me behind home plate at Target Field in Minneapolis while I sang that song in front of the largest crowd of my career. It was a moment in time that was perfectly orchestrated. The kid was able to thank the mentor for all that he had done for me. On the opposite page you'll see the great man himself, Mr. Kyle Inforzato (far left) and his beautiful wife Bonnie next to him.

COACH I AND BONNIE INFORZATO AT TARGET FIELD; JULY 5TH. 2014

Mr. Donais and Mr. Goddard. Today, as a 33-year-old professional, I consider myself an artist, musician, and performer. These are my trades. I make a living speaking on stage as a motivational speaker, and I pursue my passion as a professional singer every chance I get. I have had the good fortune to perform live for over 1,000,000 people throughout my career. In 2014, if you include the audiences on national television, my performances impacted over 17.5 million people all over the globe in a single year. All of this I owe to two men – Mr. Don Donais and Mr. Jerome Goddard. Now, they'll tell you they had nothing to do with it, but rest assured, these two men – my high school band and choir directors – are the reason I even know how to sing and perform. For these two men I have unending admiration and must express profound gratitude for the role they have played in my life. For believing in me, for mentoring me, for allowing me to dream big and pursue my goals – thank you.

--

You see, mentorship and having someone who believes in you is all you need. I have had more than my fair share of people in my young life who have been the difference makers for me. I am a lucky man indeed. But for those who may not be so fortunate, allow me to offer this example:

You need not always know the individual from whom you gather strength or inspiration on a personal level. You need not have their cell phone number or know where they live. There are people in the world who can offer their belief in you whether they know your name or not. For me, this person was Magic Johnson.

When I was 17 years old, I had the good fortune to spend a few hours with Magic as he was very generous with his time during a volunteer recognition event I was attending in Washington, D.C. On that day in May of 1999, I learned a life changing principle I have carried with me for the past 15+ years.

Magic stood in front of us and told us he never wanted to be remembered for his NBA career or for all the accolades that came with his Hall of Fame exploits on the basketball court. He taught me this:

> Magic said, "A life well-lived is a life spent giving back to those who have given so much to you."

Magic believed in our ability to live a life dedicated to giving back. Magic doesn't know who I am, nor would he remember the day we met. But for me, his words have impacted my life like few others.

MARK AND MAGIC JOHNSON – MAY 1999

Thank you for allowing me those tributes to the mentors in my life. I think it is supremely important to recognize and communicate your appreciation for those who have helped you get to where you are… and not wait until you tell the world in their eulogy so that everyone can hear it but them.

If you have a role model or mentor, tell them how much their life has meant to yours. I have highlighted a few people in my life who have helped me live a life of service to others. I truly believe that all a person needs is to have someone who is willing to believe in them; then, they will astonish you with what they can achieve.

Be that person for someone else. Mentor a young person and show them the way. Teach them how to live. Teach them to give back to others. Be a mentor. Do you want to truly serve others and impact generations to come through your service? Then, sow a seed into a young person's life by mentoring them.

To my mentors, thank you.

Everybody can be great, because anybody can serve.

Dr. Martin Luther King Jr.

Chapter 5: MLK Said It Best

Service enriches your life. Getting out into the communities and working with the people gives you a perspective that can't be duplicated by watching a YouTube video or even reading a book. I believe that service is for everyone. I believe that a service-related experience should be the foundation of every young person's life. If we desire greatness for our young people, then as Dr. King alludes – service is the way.

Allow me to take the quote to the next level. It's not only that everybody can serve; I believe that everybody should serve. In one of my TEDx Talks titled, "The Most Uninformed Decision You Will Ever Make" I promoted the idea of a Gap Year that might help young people make better decisions about their life. If you'd like to watch it, just go to YouTube and search "Mark J. Lindquist TEDx."

Just imagine if every young person in America started off their years of adulthood with a shared experience in the realm of serving others. The idea of a Gap Year has been more prevalent in the European countries than in America; but what if we in America took a little different spin on the idea? If you're not familiar with the idea of a Gap Year, the general idea is that a person would take a year of their life to do something cool before they transition into the next phase of their life. For example, a young person might choose to take a Gap Year between high school and college. During this time, a person might choose to backpack across Europe, do a missions trip overseas, travel to all 50 states, ride a bike across America, join AmeriCorps, enroll in CityYear, volunteer with the California Conservation Corps, hike the Appalachian Trail, train for and run a marathon, volunteer with a nonprofit or community organization or thousands of other creative things a person might choose to do before they embark on the next phase of their life. A student might choose to take a Gap Year after they finish their undergraduate work before they pursue their master's degree or go out into the workforce. The point is, during these times of transition, a person decides to free his- or herself up for a certain period of time to have an intentional experience that will enrich their life or simply give them a breather from the routine.

I have never been a fan of the old adage that states, "Do it while you're young!" or "Travel while you're young, and you still can!" I'm not so keen on these sayings because I believe these are limiting beliefs that somehow suggest you can't have adventures, travel and see the world once you're past a certain age. I do understand the general theme of these phrases; one certainly has to respect the challenges of picking up and traveling with a dual-income family with two kids in school and all the responsibilities that come with a modern family life. Regardless of the validity of the philosophies these phrases encapsulate, many people would agree that they should have done more traveling and adventuring when they were young. In our busy American lives, we get all wrapped up in what I call "the velocity of life" and we wake up one morning at age 35 and haven't had a vacation in over 10 years. We haven't revisited our bucket list for seemingly forever, that is, if we ever bothered to write one down.

The point is, our lives get busy, and we end up having to wait until retirement to take the grand adventures we wish we would have when we were young. Since I believe we live in a society with a generation of young people who simply aren't willing to wait until they're 68 years old to have adventures in their life - the Gap Year is a perfect addition to the lives of the millennial generation and beyond.

Here's an idea I'd like to suggest for a new generation of young Americans. Let's take the example of the National Basketball Association (NBA). [1]In 2005, the NBA Players Association and the NBA reached a collective bargaining agreement that established a new rule stating that a player would not be eligible for the NBA draft unless they turned 19 years of age during the calendar year of that year's draft. The league stated, "The need to see players perform against higher competition before they are evaluated for valuable draft picks." As a sports fan myself, I just figured that the NBA was trying to encourage young athletes to go to college as a viable option for their future instead of relying on becoming the next Kevin Garnett or LeBron James.

Think about what the NBA has done. If you're a star basketball player who is 17 or 18 years old when you graduate high school, and you're not eligible for the NBA draft until you turn 19, then what are your options? You could continue to play on the playgrounds and in the pick-up games at the YMCA, or you could go to college and develop your game there for at least a year.

What if American society adopted a similar requirement for admission into college? My belief is that two things happen during your first year of college:

1. You lose your head. You're so excited about living on your own outside of mom and dad's rules and influence that you go absolutely bananas your first year of school. For some, it's going overboard at parties. For others, it's simply hanging out with friends until 3 a.m. For me, it was hanging out with my buddies

Jake, Steve, Alex and Nate while eating copious amounts of pizza, playing video games and falling asleep on their futon to a late night viewing of the David Spade and Chris Farley classic "Tommy Boy." Did I go to class the next day? Nah. I hadn't yet learned the skills that allowed me to control and manage this newfound freedom that was freshman college life.

2. You learn very little that you remember today. Here's the test. Prepare a three-minute presentation on one of the things that you learned in class during your freshman year of college. Go ahead.

Do it now.

I'm still waiting.

Come on.

Your average texting conversation probably lasts longer than three minutes, and your latest visit to Facebook or your Words With Friends game on your phone lasted longer than three minutes for sure.

But I'll bet many of you couldn't come up with three minutes of material on something you paid thousands of dollars for during the 18th and 19th year of your life.

What if American society followed the lead of the NBA and didn't admit students into their freshman year of college until they were 19?

Take those thousands of dollars you spent on your freshman year and go out and hike to the top of Pikes Peak and feel your lungs gasp for oxygen above 14,000 feet. Take a train ride to Munich and experience an Oktoberfest like none other. Go float in a gondola on the Grand Canal in Venice and eat a slice of pizza made in an Italian kitchen. Go have an adventure of your choice. Show up at the airport, ask them where the planes are headed that day and jump on one. Get lost in a city. Ride the trains. Get in a cab in Paris and start speaking English to the cab driver and see if he'll take you to the place you want to go. (Seriously, I've done that. It's hilarious!)

Let's say you did even one of those things when you were 18 or 19 years old. Now prepare a three-minute presentation on one of the things you did during that Gap Year.

I'll bet you'd have a hard time whittling it down to three minutes.

You could probably tell stories for an entire afternoon about the adventures you had, the scary and insecure moments you experienced and the funny things that happened. At the end of your year, you've been outside your hometown. You've been away from the things that are familiar. You've grown as a person. You've increased your knowledge of self and your surroundings. Your perspective on life has been broadened. You're a better version of you.

Now go off to college and begin making these decisions about what you want to do with your life. Now you are better equipped to make decisions about the kind of life you want to live and possibly the impact you want to have on the world around you.

But think… we haven't even entertained the idea of the impact this Gap Year may have on our lives if we chose to use that year as a year of service to others. What if you served in the nonprofit sector or for a community organization or in the U.S. Military during that time? What if you worked in a homeless shelter or soup kitchen or tutored inner-city school kids during that year? Wouldn't every single decision you make for the rest of your life be of a higher quality because you have broadened your horizons and have a greater understanding of the needs of the world around you?

Also, think about the experience of "service" in a different way. Jared, my long-time friend who is now my business partner, always says that he thinks each and every person in the world should be made to have a job as a waiter/waitress or work a customer service job sometime early in their lives. Why? Because then maybe the next time your order was a little cold or you got regular Coke instead of Diet Coke, you wouldn't treat the human being who is working at that establishment like they were your indentured servant – and maybe you'd treat them more like they're a human who is just as imperfect as you are.

When I think about service and giving back to others and the perspective it gives me – I liken it to the experience of being made to be a "server" at a restaurant. Now, because I know what it is like to be on the other side of the table – I make decisions that are more compassionate and forgiving, choosing first to care for my fellow man rather than judge them.

Take this for example. Many of my friends over the years have made comments about the panhandler on the highway exit or the street corner and how it disgusts them that they even exist. They cite some ridiculous story they read on the Internet about how most of these "bums" make more money begging on the street corner than we do at a minimum wage job. They laugh it off and move on to the next mundane conversation. They have this perspective about a fellow human being and a social ill that exists in their community because that is exactly what they lack… perspective.

When I see a seemingly homeless person on the sidewalk or on the street corner, I think of something different than most. I recall a chilly night in Washington, D.C. when I was 19 years old, and I had just enrolled in AmeriCorps, a volunteer service program much like a "domestic Peace Corps." It gets cold in D.C. in the winter, and we were downtown for a community project during the day when I saw a homeless person huddled in a blanket on the sidewalk. I am from a town of 2,000 people, and I grew up on a farm in western Minnesota. At age 19, this was the very first time I had seen a homeless person sleeping on a sidewalk.

It bothered me to no end. My world was shaken. As a young person, figuring out the world and learning things for the first time, it was hard for me to be faced with this reality. I couldn't get it out of my mind for days, so I decided to do something about it. I took the #2 bus to the store, and I used what little money I had to buy some spaghetti, some sauce and a few pounds of hamburger. I took it back to our AmeriCorps campus, and I cooked it up and placed it in some Tupperware. I wasn't much of a cook, but this is what I could do. I grabbed some bread and sealed it up in a bag, and I walked out the door. I had borrowed my buddy Ryan's car, and I didn't tell anybody where I was going that night.

I parked the car around G Street and got out of the car with my backpack full of food. I wandered the cold and bitter streets for a while until I finally found the person I had seen a few days earlier. He was wearing a worn and tattered brown coat, and he had a hooded sweatshirt over his head. He and a few other men and women were huddled together under some old sleeping bags next to an office building overhang. I gently walked up to the man and said:

"Hi. Would you like some food?"

I reached in my backpack and took out a container of spaghetti and meat sauce, and I handed it to him. He looked up at me with amazement as he received the Tupperware container, and he said to the woman next to him:

"Wow. It's still warm."

I reached in my backpack again and pulled out a bag of bread and a few forks I had scrounged up from around our campus and handed them to him.

His eyes told the story. It was like he couldn't believe I had bread and forks too.

"Thank you… thank you," He said.

As I turned to leave, a thought popped into my head.

He doesn't have any gloves. It's freezing out here, and his hands were ice cold to the touch. I paused for a brief second and felt a wave of selfishness pass over me. You see, these were my favorite gloves. My mom had purchased them for me before I left for D.C. in the fall.

With a bit of reluctance and a feeling of guilt that I had been so selfish, I turned back and asked the man if he would like some gloves.

He didn't know what to say. I pulled my gloves off my hands and handed them to him.

"God Bless You… God Bless You," He said.

As I walked away that chilly D.C. night, it was probably one of the most satisfying, heartwarming and profound experiences I had ever had in my 19 years of life on this earth. I remember being upset afterward, when someone had found out what I did that night. I didn't do it for recognition or praise. I did it because I couldn't get the thought out of my head that a human being was going to crawl up inside a worn out sleeping bag and shiver in the cold sidewalk that night. I don't know his story. I don't know if he made good decisions or bad decisions. I don't know, and I don't care.

But now, when I see a homeless person on the side of the road, I think of that night in D.C. I recall the look in his eyes when I gave him what was maybe the first warm meal of that cold winter. I learned a lot on that night too. I remember thinking when I was in the kitchen… "Man, I would hate to eat a plate of spaghetti without a piece of bread." So I threw some bread in my bag. At the very last minute, it hit me that he probably wouldn't have a way to eat the meal without a fork.

Treat other people the way you would want to be treated, right? I learned that lesson when I was 19 years old, serving in AmeriCorps. My classroom was a cold street in D.C. on a night where there was no teacher and no syllabus. I learned a lesson

I have carried with me for the past 14 years, and I can tell you all about it today. It was one of the most important lessons of my life. It happened during my Gap Year when I purposely set out to serve others.

On that night, my life was great.

It is true. Everybody can be great, because anybody can serve.

---

1. "ARTICLE X - PLAYER ELIGIBILITY AND NBA DRAFT." 2005 Collective Bargaining Agreement (2005): 225-36. NBA Players. National Basketball Players Association, 16 Dec. 2009. Web. 26 Feb. 2015.

Chapter 6: Corporate Community Involvement

There is a buzzword that has been building its reputation in the corporate world for the past 15 years or so. It's called "Corporate Community Involvement." Here's how it was explained to me a dozen years ago:

Corporations are beginning to understand that when the buying public sees your company doing good in the community, it positively affects your bottom line. The concise version boils it down to the following. For example, let's say that a customer has the option to shop at Company A or Company B. If the customer knows that Company A contributes resources and manpower to local community gardening and green spaces around the area and Company B does not, then the customer may be more likely to support Company A simply because they give back to the community.

This phenomenon is why you'll walk into a Target store and on the front wall near the cash registers, you'll see a big sign that says, "Target contributes over $1,000,000 to schools every week." Or at the front of every Wal-Mart you shop in, you'll see a running tally of how much that local store has contributed to the community since January 1st of that year. The general idea is that even a big corporation can do well by doing good.

When I came on the scene in 2003 and began working for a national nonprofit organization called "KaBoom!" I was just learning about this shift in the corporate world. If you remember back in the early part of the last decade, the corporate world was getting hammered in the media for all the scandals and wrongdoing going on behind closed doors. First it was the Enron debacle; then it was Tyco; followed by Martha Stewart. In general, these stories painted a rather grim picture of Corporate America and its ability to maintain our trust.

In response to this decline in corporate trust, many major companies established what we call "Corporate Community Involvement" (CCI) departments. The basic marching orders were to have employees go out into the community and do good things. Wear a t-shirt with our company logo on it. Choose a cause that aligns with our mission or, at the very least, our employee's favorite charities. We'll throw a couple million dollars at it every year, and maybe the public will believe in Corporate America again. That was the general idea being tossed around the executive suites of Fortune 500 companies in the early part of the 2000's, and I was lucky enough to be right in the middle of it all.

After my AmeriCorps term of service, I chose to go work for the largest playground building nonprofit in the country. One of the early leaders of this CCI movement was our organization "KaBoom!" Our model was awesome. The CEO, Darrell Hammond, developed a single-day blitz-build model whereby a corporate sponsor would donate money and send employees to a local inner-city community and partner with a community organization like Boys and Girls Club or YMCA to erect a playground in a day. It was a magnificent process that partnered corporate employees with residents of underserved communities for probably the first time in that community's history. I would be flown into the neighborhood two or three months before the event to sit with a group of kids and design the playground of their dreams. We would sit around knee high tables, draw with color crayons and imagine the new playground that they would soon have to play on. I would take those drawings and shop them around the manufacturer catalog trying to align the kids' wishes with an actual playground component they asked for. Two months later, I would fly back to that community and lead a single-day blitz build with the help of over 100 corporate employees and 50-100 community members. It was magical. In the morning, we'd look out on the build site and see nothing but a pile of dirt. By mid-afternoon, there was a beautiful brand new playground built by people who lived and worked in that community. For the next 30 years, they could drive by that site and see something accomplished because we brought together business people to work alongside inner-city residents and their families. What an awesome process to be a part of.

At the same time, while I was busy working on playgrounds in almost every major city in America, the White House was busy working on an initiative called "Business Strengthening America" that would unite Fortune 500 CEO's like Steve Case of AOL/Time Warner, Jeff Swartz from Timberland and Ken Thompson of Wachovia to dedicate themselves and their companies to the cause of serving their communities. For example, Ken Thompson's Wachovia managed a great program for their employees whereby an employee could take a certain amount of paid company time and volunteer in the community at certain places and within certain categories of service. It was all part of an initiative within the corporate world to improve the image of these major companies while doing something good for people.

My point in sharing all of this about the CCI movement in America is to encourage other companies to follow the lead of those early-adopters I just mentioned. If we in the nonprofit and community organization sector of America are going to accomplish the things that we truly want to… we are going to need the assistance – nay,

partnership with Corporate America to get these things done. Not only will we need the resources that Corporate America brings to the table, but also, we will need their influence, talent and ingenuity.

"*People are weary of being asked to do the least they can possibly do. People are yearning to measure the full distance of their potential on behalf of the causes they care about deeply. But they have to be asked.*"

Dan Pallotta
HUMANITARIAN ACTIVIST AND
FOUNDER OF PALLOTTA TEAMWORKS

Chapter 7: Dan Pallotta Is a Genius

Dan Pallotta did a TED Talk, and it is the best 18 minutes and 54 seconds that you will ever hear on the future of the nonprofit sector. His TED Talk is titled, "The Way We Think About Charity is Dead Wrong." Google it. YouTube it. Watch it.

I know this is a book and you can't click on this link… but I am so in love with this TED Talk, I just want to make sure you have every avenue to be able to watch it.

Dan Pallotta's TED Talk: http://youtu.be/bfAzi6D5FpM

Oh, and if you still can't get the video for some reason, email me personally at mark@breathislimited.com, and I'll send you the link.

I hope you get my point. Watch this 18-minute video. It will change the way you think about charity and charitable organizations for the rest of your life.

And that's the end of this chapter. ☺

"Ask not what your country can do for you,
ask what you can do for your country."

John F. Kennedy
INAUGURATION ADDRESS, JANUARY 1961

Chapter 8: JFK's Words Today

My vision for America is more complex than simply yearning for the days of old when things were simpler and front porches were the social network of the day. My vision for America consists of an engaged and zealous generation of young citizens who stand in ardent support of the life they have imagined and will not back down until they discover their authentic self and their place in the world. I believe this generation of young Americans has something to say about the playbook we have been handed. I believe the system we are expected to follow is not the one we would follow if given the freedom to choose.

Thoreau says that if we advance confidently in the direction of our dreams and endeavor to live the life we have imagined, then we will achieve success unexpected in common hours. I believe that our dreams are to own our life and not submit them 40 hours a week to a cubicle. I believe young Americans see what is possible in the palm of their hand as they watch a YouTube video of adventures being had and exciting lives being lived on the other end of the camera that captured it. I believe we see the possibilities of life in our newsfeeds and in our inboxes, and we have an unquenchable thirst to go live our lives to the fullest and express who we are so the world can see it. The greatest parts of humanity are shown to us on a daily basis at the click of a button and a Google search, and we have a visceral desire see the best of life in our own reality as well as on TV. I believe I am a part of a generation that is ready to change the way life is lived and redefine the significance of that dash between the dates on our headstone.

We want more. We demand more. We will be more.

One of the ways I believe we will do this is by extending ourselves in the name of service to such a degree that one day an esteemed member of our society will write a book as Tom Brokaw did and call us the Greatest Generation. Now is our time. Now is our time to stand up and make the words of the great man ring true through every heart and mind throughout our nation.

We are the generation who must stand up and say:

Ask not what the world can do for you; ask what you are willing to do to serve the world.

Service. It is my way of life.

Epilogue

If I could help be the change I wish to see in America, I would start with these three:
1. Change the service club modus operandi
2. Advocate for service-based Gap Years becoming the new normal in our society
3. Get behind businesses engaging on a massive level to solve social problems throughout America and the world

I truly believe that if my generation is going to create a society worthy of our signature, some of the transformations inside that society are listed above.

1. If you are a person who sees large-scale change throughout America, you're going to need the civic organizations to come forward with a grassroots effort to help implement your ideas. Organizations such as Kiwanis, Lions, Rotary, Sertoma, Optimists, PTA, Knights of Columbus, VFW, American Legion and so many others are an integral part to the way communities across our nation address problems and serve people. I am deeply concerned, along with the rest of my service club comrades, about the future of our organizations and our ability to survive and thrive through the middle part of the 21st

century. Although I don't believe the plan I have outlined in Chapter 3 of this book is necessarily a perfectly conceived plan without shortcomings, it is a plan I believe we must migrate toward over the course of the next decade, or we will find our membership rosters decimated and our influence diminished. These organizations represent the foundation of my life; it was inside the Kiwanis family I learned the values I hold dear to my heart today. What I desire is for future generations of young people to be able to experience the same mentorship, inspiration, leadership challenges and service opportunities I was able to experience when I was in my late teens.

2. When I took off for AmeriCorps in the fall of 2000, I didn't know I was a taking a "Gap Year" – I didn't even know what a Gap Year was. I only knew I was called to serve my fellow man, and I got on a plane and committed myself to the cause. Because of my willingness to get outside of my comfort zone and travel to unknown places in the name of service to others, I was able to have a life enriching experience that positively shaped the next 15 years of my life. I can truly say – without that Gap Year, the life I have lived would be 180 degrees in the opposite direction, and I am certain I would not be the passionate, authentic person I am today. I believe this foundational and shared experience is crucial to the success of a young

person's development and progression in a global society; and in my eyes I define that success as one arriving at the destination of becoming the authentic version of you. No matter if you achieve this characterization at age 22 or 32 or 52... this is the destination at which I desire so many other people to arrive. To live life as the authentic version of you is in my opinion the only way to live. The destination is worth the trials of the journey. Choose a Gap Year that will assist you in the discovery of the authentic you.

3. In the realm of nonprofits and community organizations, if we are to accomplish the things and solve the problems we aspire to, we must develop a more robust partnership with Corporate America and the resources that lie within. In order to tackle the major social problems of our time we must take heed to Dan Pallotta's wisdom as presented in his TED Talk. With charitable giving stuck at 2 percent of Gross Domestic Product in the U.S., we need the support of the corporate world to move that needle so the nonprofit organizations that are doing such great work in our country have the resources necessary to solve the problems they dedicate their lives to.

I believe this is our time. This is my generation's time to start shaping the definition the history books will label us with. The millennials are far more than just our iPhones, our laptops and our social media. We are a people who long for something more, something real, something that makes an impact, something that moves us. You won't capture our attention in the ways that previous generations have been enthralled – and that's not a criticism of those who have gone before us. It is simply an accurate description of how my generation makes you fight for our gaze. We want to make an impact, and we want to change lives – we just need a compelling reason to do so when faced with all the distractions of modern life in the early part of the 21st century.

We're faced with a dilemma in 2015. Continue on the path that is comfortable, safe and cozy – or look outside our own bubble and recognize that now is the time to do something for the world. Now is the time to take advantage of the opportunity to impact the lives of those around us. Now is the time to make **Service, Our Way of Life.**

Making Our Impact on the World

I give my passionate self to the world as often as I possibly can. As a motivational speaker, entertainer and entrepreneur I seek to make my impact on the world in many ways. Primarily, I deliver keynote speeches at conferences and conventions, for corporate meetings and employee gatherings. I also deliver school assemblies at middle and high schools, and I speak at youth conferences, colleges and Young Professionals Networks. Another one of my passions is found in the realm of volunteerism; for that reason I also speak for nonprofit groups, civic organizations and service clubs.

My business manager, long-time best friend and like-minded champion of passion, Mr. Jared L. Bye, is the one who makes all of this happen. He is truly the "brains behind our operation" and makes it possible for our companies to make the impact that they do. We speak to people as young as 5th graders all the way up to the CEO's and business leaders at billion dollar companies. When we are out on the road and on stage, you'll find us delivering keynotes on three different topics:

Passion. Leadership. Service.

At Breath Is Limited Motivational Speaking, LLC, we are in the business of "Advancing Ideas… Igniting Passion." Our goal is to lead as many people as possible toward the discovery of their passions. We seek to inspire, entertain and lead others toward their passionate self.

Here is our full topic list as of February of 2015:
Also found at www.BreathIsLimited.com

Passion! 8 Steps to Find Yours

Based on our smash hit book "Passion! 8 Steps to Find Yours," Mark will deliver a talk packed with fun and overflowing with excitement about how to live a life filled with passion. Whether you're wondering how to rediscover your passionate self in the workplace or you're hoping to find the things you love during your off hours - "Passion! 8 Steps to Find Yours" is for you. Audience members will have the opportunity to hear Mark teach straight from the playbook he has developed in 26 countries and all 50 states. Suitable for Corporate Audiences, Conference Keynotes, Young Professionals Networks, College Audiences and School Assemblies.

Service, My Way of Life

This keynote is perfect for the organization experiencing employee burnout and volunteer fatigue or the company that has a stressed out workforce. Mark uses his vast experience serving in 22 countries and 44 states in the nonprofit community, with community organizations, the U.S. Military, the Department of Homeland Security and AmeriCorps to communicate an inspiring message to your people that will leave them ready to recommit themselves to your cause. Following this talk, your audiences will be ready to go out and change the world. Suitable for Corporate Audiences, Conference Keynotes, Civic Organizations, Youth Groups, School Assemblies and Corporate Community Involvement Departments.

Gratitude. Live it.

During this riveting keynote address, Mark will inject a profound sense of gratitude into your organizational culture and leave your people with a common language to build upon. Mark will provide a toolkit of ideas that will help a person carry their gratitude with them into the future. Following this talk, audience members have called loved ones they haven't called for years; individuals who weren't on speaking terms found a way to mend fences and move forward. Mark will have your people diving down into the deepest roots of themselves - and at the end of the day, your people will be undeniably changed. Suitable for Corporate Audiences,

Conference Keynotes, School Assemblies and Classroom Presentations.

The 7 Mindsets to Live Your Ultimate Life
Want to know how the most successful and happy people got to where they are? "The 7 Mindsets to Live Your Ultimate Life" (Written by Scott Shickler and Jeff Waller) are the result of a multi-year, multi-million dollar research project that uncovered the key component of a person's success and happiness: Their Mindset. Mark will teach you how to live what we call, "Your Ultimate Life." Suitable for Corporate Audiences, School Assemblies, Full and Half-Day Training for Youth and Adults.

Opportunity Ahead
Mark has been more places and has experienced more incredible things than most have ever dreamed of. Allow this world-touring entertainer, Hollywood actor, nationally recognized singer, author and motivational speaker to show you the opportunities that exist in your life. This is a show-stopping talk about finding your passion and seizing opportunities meant for you. Suitable for Corporate Audiences, Conference Keynotes, Young Professionals Networks and School Assemblies.

Own the Stage

This keynote will be THE professional development event of your year! We have all attended the excruciatingly boring meetings with the same old 1990s power point. Mark has performed live for over 1,000,000 people throughout his career in audiences around the globe. He has performed for staffers at the White House and at NATO Headquarters in Europe, as well as for NFL players, Major League Baseball, the NCAA and the NHL. Mark will pass on his vast experience, rehearsal tips, techniques, strategies to own the crowd and presentation knowledge that will make you look like a pro. Suitable for anyone seeking an entertaining and engaging professional development opportunity.

Feeling Norwegian – Growing Up Asian in Small Town Minnesota

Mark shares his journey through a world where everyone around him expected the book to match the cover. Meaning, they expected him to act a certain way or have a certain viewpoint simply because he looked Asian. This talk is as insightful as it is entertaining as Mark chronicles the hilarious although sometimes painful experience of being the only minority in the room – often being expected to speak on behalf of an entire race of people. During this hour of fun and self-reflection, Mark will have your audience rolling in the aisles about our preconceived notions about people, but at the same time, he'll have your people reflecting deeply about what it means to be the only minority in the room your entire life.

As a successful businessman who immigrated to this country years ago, Mark will share his victories and trials with your audience and open up his playbook of success so that they can live a happy and passionate life no matter where they came from or what they look like.

Suitable for college campuses, student organizations and Multicultural and Diversity offices.

" What happens if we invest in developing our people and then they leave us? "

" What happens if we don't and they stay? "

Breath Is Limited Conference Services
The compliment we most often receive is, "Mark was the best hour of our conference!" Allow us to make your entire event, "The best conference in decades."

We offer:
- Keynotes
- Breakout Sessions
- Half-Day Trainings
- World-Class Emceeing
- Live Sinatra-Style Entertainment (Solo, 60-90 Minute Set)
- Live Sinatra-Style Entertainment (Live 16 Piece Band, 60-90 Minute Set)

Few speakers can make an impact at your upcoming conference in the many ways Mark J. Lindquist can.

Find us at www.BreathIsLimited.com!

About the Co-Author Mark J. Lindquist

Mark J. Lindquist is a nationally recognized speaker and world-touring entertainer who has performed live for over **one million people** throughout his career. As an actor, he has appeared in the ABC drama "LOST," the CBS remake of "Hawaii Five-O" and the Universal Studios movie "Battleship." He has performed for Grammy-winning artists, Academy Award-nominated actors and foreign dignitaries around the world, as well as staffers at the White House. Mark has been featured on CNN.com, C-Span, The Washington Post, The Washington Times, The San Francisco Chronicle, The Houston Chronicle, The Miami Herald and the Korea Today Newspaper (Seoul, South Korea).

Mark has shared the stage with former U.S. Attorney General Janet Reno; Senator John McCain; Magic Johnson; Edward James Olmos; Grammy Award-winning artists Rihanna, Brooks and Dunn and Brandy; Academy Award-nominated Actor Liam Neeson; as well as CEOs Bob Nardelli (Home Depot), Steve Case (AOL/Time Warner), Ken Thompson (Wachovia), Jeff Swartz (Timberland) and Ben and Jerry (Ben and Jerry's Ice Cream).

Throughout his entertainment career, Mark has performed for the Tuskegee Airmen, the Secretary of the Interior Gayle Norton, Secretary of Commerce Don Evans, Secretary of Labor Elaine

Chao, Members of Congress, Sargent Shriver, Mia Hamm, Tony Stewart, the Washington Nationals (MLB), the NCAA, Universal Studios and the Supreme Allied Commander of NATO Europe. Mark has also performed in 22 countries and 44 states and has toured the world as an entertainer and emcee.

Currently, Mark travels the country performing the National Anthem for collegiate and professional sports teams, and he delivers keynote addresses for businesses, associations, conferences and school assemblies. He is the fulltime National Anthem singer for the University of North Dakota Men's Hockey Program and a guest performer for the College World Series, the Minnesota Twins, the Los Angeles Dodgers and the Minnesota Vikings.

Mark co-founded Breath Is Limited Motivational Speaking, LLC with Jared L. Bye as their way of bringing a message of hope, passion, perseverance and joy to people all over the world. Mark is a former Sergeant in the United States Air Force and an Afghanistan War Veteran who grew up in Ortonville, Minnesota.

Mark currently lives in Fargo, North Dakota.

Mark J. Lindquist

Jared L. Bye

About the Co-Author Jared L. Bye

Jared L. Bye is an entrepreneur who currently owns, controls and manages Breath is Limited Motivational Speaking and Entertainment as well as a life insurance agency based out of Fargo, North Dakota.

In his role at Breath is Limited Motivational Speaking and Entertainment, Jared represents clients throughout the United States. He consults with speakers and entertainers, negotiates contracts on the client's behalf and books gigs for the speaker/entertainer after a brief probationary period. Jared works with speakers who are brand new to the business as well as seasoned veterans of the stage. No matter the level of experience, Jared's managerial expertise has proven to be an invaluable component of a performer's success.

As Mark J. Lindquist's business manager, Jared is the co-author of this book as well as "Passion! 8 Steps to Find Yours," he is a marketing consultant, and lead speechwriter who co-wrote two TED Talks since 2013. Together, they impacted over 17.5 million people with their work in the year 2014.

Contacting Mark, Jared and Breath Is Limited Motivational Speaking:

You can contact the business office at Breath Is Limited Motivational Speaking, LLC at:

3120-Z 25th Street South
Suite 160
Fargo, ND 58103

You may email us at:
Mark@BreathIsLimited.com
Jared@BreathIsLimited.com

Websites: www.BreathIsLimited.com
                www.MarkJLindquist.com

Twitter: @MarkJLindquist
Facebook: Mark J. Lindquist
Instagram: MarkJLindquist
LinkedIn: Mark J. Lindquist

Service! My Way of Life.

25731317R00069

Made in the USA
San Bernardino, CA
10 November 2015